BOOKIES

Bookmarks to Crochet

Jonas Matthies

Dover Publications, Inc.
Mineola, New York

Bibliographical Note

This Dover edition, first published in 2019, is a new English translation of the original
German edition published as *bookies* by topp–kreativ, Stuttgart, Germany, in 2018.
This edition is published by arrangement with Claudia Böhme Rights & Literary Agency,
Hannover, Germany (www.agency-boehme.com).

Library of Congress Cataloging-in-Publication Data

Names: Matthies, Jonas, author.
Title: Bookies : bookmarks to crochet / Jonas Matthies.
Other titles: Bookies. English
Description: Mineola, New York : Dover Publications, Inc., 2019. |
    Translation of: Bookies : Tierische Lesezeichen zum Häkeln. Stuttgart,
    Germany : by topp-kreativ, 2018.
Identifiers: LCCN 2018054006| ISBN 9780486833941 | ISBN 0486833941
Subjects: LCSH: Bookmarks. | Crocheting—Patterns.
Classification: LCC TT825 .M34 2019 | DDC 746.43/4—dc23
LC record available at https://lccn.loc.gov/2018054006

Manufactured in the United States by LSC Communications
83394101   2019
www.doverpublications.com

Jonas Matthies

...Mr. Supergurumi loves to travel

Hello, dear crochet friends.

My name is Jonas, and I was born and raised in Berlin. I first found my way to crochet after many years of traveling. I didn't go to college after graduating high school. Instead, I spent half a year in faraway Thailand. After that, I knew that I wanted to devote my future to traveling the world rather than spending my time in lecture halls. I was already interested in web design and marketing, so I decided to broaden my knowledge in those fields to support my life abroad. And so, within a few years, I said goodbye to Germany and settled into my new life.

Over the years, while researching extensively online for new projects, I noticed the enormous interest in specialty communities for *amigurumi* (the Japanese art of crocheting small creatures). I was immediately delighted by the variety of imaginative creations in this field. Initially I tried to find an author to create an amigurumi project. But I soon realized how difficult it is to have your ideas implemented by others. And that's how it all started!

At this time I was settled in Bali, and I ordered a giant package of wool and every piece of crochet equipment I could think of. After a relatively rough start, I managed to create my own little amigurumi, which I published on my website www.Supergurumi.com.
Over time, my figures and tutorials became more and more popular. I decided to combine my web interest with amigurumi.

As an avid reader, I never have enough bookmarks. So I came up with the idea to crochet one—but not just an ordinary bookmark. No, I wanted a bookmark that fit more with the amigurumi theme. One day, I saw one of Bali's countless geckos sitting on my hammock, and the idea for my first bookmark was born. I published the Book Rat and the Book Gecko and received superfriendly, positive feedback. What fun I had, translating my ideas into crochet animals!

I never thought that this initial idea would become an entire book, one that I hope is not only fun to crochet with, but also a joy to read.

I would like to thank all the readers of this book as well as visitors to my website. Only through your encouragement and feedback was it possible for crochet to become an integral part of my life. I'm grateful for that and also for the opportunity to share my ideas with you, no matter where I find myself in the world.

Have fun!

Yours,

Jonas Matthies

Contents

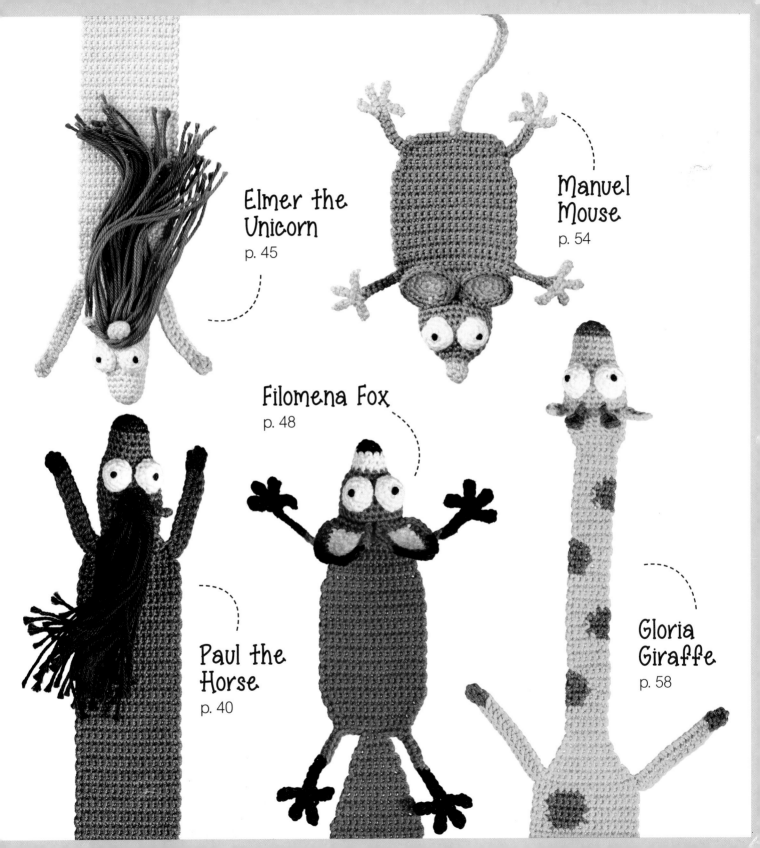

Elmer the
Unicorn
p. 45

Manuel
Mouse
p. 54

Filomena Fox
p. 48

Paul the
Horse
p. 40

Gloria
Giraffe
p. 58

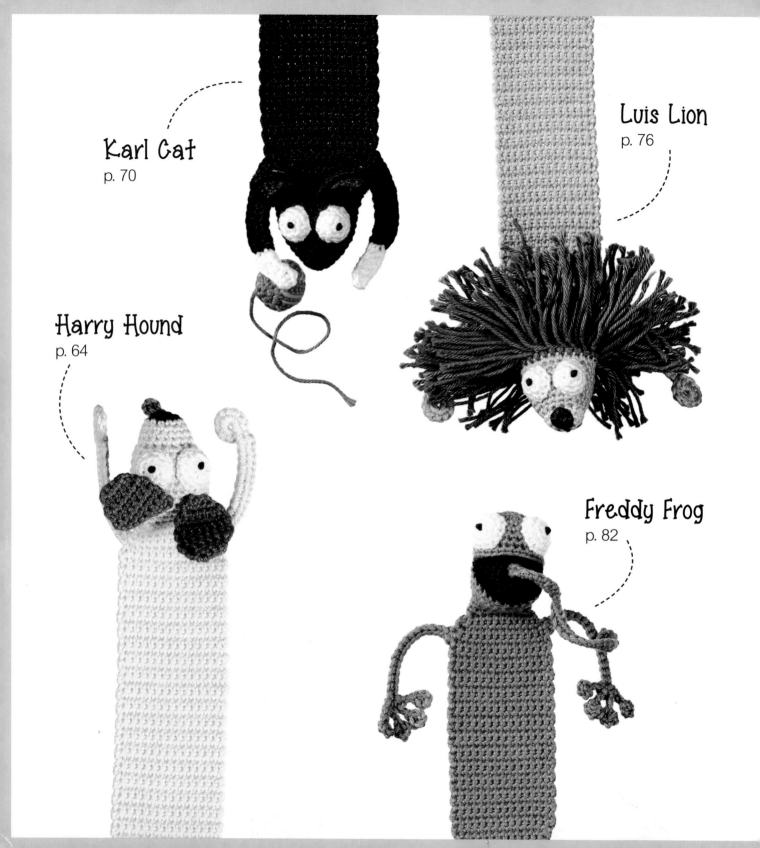

Karl Cat
p. 70

Luis Lion
p. 76

Harry Hound
p. 64

Freddy Frog
p. 82

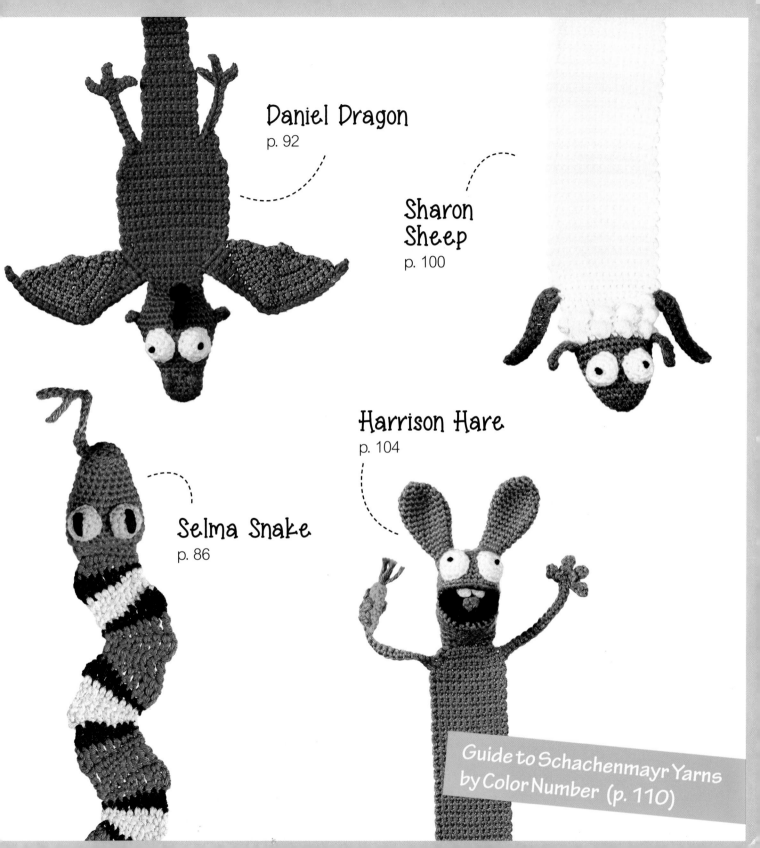

Daniel Dragon
p. 92

Sharon
Sheep
p. 100

Harrison Hare
p. 104

Selma Snake
p. 86

Guide to Schachenmayr Yarns by Color Number (p. 110)

Crochet Head Together

1 Hold the HEAD so that you have two rows, one on top of the other, with the same amount of sts. The last–worked st should be all the way to the right.

2 Insert the hook through the next st on the bottom and the one directly above it on the top, so the hook is through two sts. Wrap the yarn and pull through both sts.

3 Continue working the remaining sts in this way, following the specific instructions in the pattern, until all of the sts are crocheted together.

Eyes (2X)

Variation 1

Work the EYES in White in a spiral round.

Rnd 1: 5sc in a magic ring (5).

Rnd 2: 2sc in each st (10).

Rnd 3: 10sc (10).

Rnd 4: 2sc.

Cut the yarn, leaving a long tail, and pull it through the last st to fasten off.

Variation 2

Rnd 1: 6sc in a magic ring (6).

Rnd 2: 2sc in each st (12).

Rnd 3: 12sc (12).

Rnd 4: 2sc.

Cut the yarn, leaving a long tail, and pull it through the last st to fasten off.

Variation 3

Rnd 1: 5sc in a magic ring (5).

Rnd 2: 2sc in each st (10).

Rnd 3: 10sc (10).

Rnd 4: Change color to Coffee and work the next rnd through the back loop. 2sc in each st (20).

Begin to work in rows.

Rows 1–3: 5sc, ch1 (4).

Row 4: [sc2tog] 2x (2).

Cut the yarn, leaving a long tail, and pull it through the last st to fasten off.

Pupils

Take a long strand of Black yarn and wrap the ends over each other to form a circle. Weave one end through the circle 3x and pull closed to make a knot. Thread both ends through a yarn needle and pull through the middle of the EYE, knotting closed multiple times on the other side to secure. Trim ends.

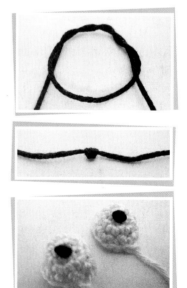

Basic Techniques

Materials for Bookies

All of the Bookies were crocheted using *Catania* by Schachenmayr (1.5oz/50g balls, 136yds/125m). This 100% cotton yarn is wonderful to work with, has a slight sheen, and comes in a large variety of colors. Since you only need a small amount of yarn for each project, smaller scraps will usually be enough. **For a guide to the numbers that correspond to each color used in this book, please see page 110.**

You will also need the following materials:

2.5mm crochet hook

Yarn needle

Stuffing (Polyester filling)

Scissors

Gauge

With a 2.5mm crochet hook, 10sc and 11 rows = 3cm x 3cm

[3cm = 1.2in]

Basic Knowledge

Slipknot

The slipknot is the starting point of every piece of crochet. To begin, take the yarn in your left hand.

1 Take the yarn between your little finger and ring finger from front to back, then behind the hand to the pointer finger. Wrap it around the pointer finger from back to front. Wrap the yarn around the thumb from front to back and hold the end with your other three fingers. The yarn should cross over itself between the thumb and pointer fingers.

2 Insert the hook from bottom to top in the thumb loop. Hook the yarn coming off the pointer finger and pull through the thumb loop, letting go of the thumb loop once the hook is through.

3 Pull the yarn to tighten the slipknot until it lies snugly against the hook.

Chain (ch)

A chain stitch is the stitch that is always needed in crochet. It's often used at the beginning of the work, or at the beginning of a row or round, or strung together as a mesh or web within a pattern.

1 Hold the end of the yarn directly below the slipknot. For the 1st ch, wrap the working yarn around the hook, or slide the hook underneath the yarn.

2 Pull the yarn through the slipknot to make the first ch st.

3 Continue working in this manner to keep making chain sts—that is, wrap the yarn again and pull it through the loop on the hook to form the next st. When counting ch sts, do not count the loop on your hook.

Single Crochet (sc)

The stitch pattern for single crochet is relatively dense and looks very decorative thanks to its simple structure.

1 To work a sc in the next st, insert hook into the st, wrap the yarn around the hook, and pull it through, pulling the new loop to the same height as the loop on your hook. You should have 2 loops on your hook.

2 Wrap the yarn and pull through both loops. The sc st will look like a little "v."

13

Crochet in the row

Every piece of crochet that will lie flat begins with a chain, and the first row is crocheted into this chain.

To reach the correct height for the next row, rows begin with ch sts. The number of ch sts depends on the type of st being worked:

sc = ch1
hdc = ch2
dc = ch3
tr = ch4

This also means, for example, that if you're working a row of sc, the 1st st in the beginning chain must be worked in the 2nd st from the hook. If you were working a row of dc, the 1st st would have to be worked in the 4th st from the hook.

1 At the end of the row, turn the work so that all of the sts are on the left side of the hook.

2 To make it easier to turn the work, you can work the ch sts first. You can also work the ch sts after turning. To begin a new row, work in the 1st st in the row below, which is marked here.

3 Work the 3rd and all following rows in this manner.

Magic Ring

1 Wrap the yarn around your hand as shown in the photo. At the same time, wrap the working yarn once, counter-clockwise, around your thumb. Hold the end yarn beneath the middle, ring, and pinky fingers.

2 Insert the hook from top to bottom below the thumb strand and pull through the pointer–finger strand. You'll have a loop on your hook. Catch the strand again . . .

3 . . . and pull it through the loop. The yarn is now doubled on the left side of the thumb and single on the right side.

4 Work 1sc around the doubled yarn.

5 Pull your thumb out of the loop. Continue working sts around the doubled loop, until you reach the desired number of sts.

6 To close, hold the end yarn in your left hand and the work in your right hand, and pull the end yarn snugly. There will be a tiny hole in the center.

Spiral Round

When working in a spiral round, the work is not turned at the end of the round. As such, you're always working on the right side of the work. With this technique, your rounds do not "end." The 1st st of the next round is simply worked over the 1st st of the previous round, thereby creating a spiral.

Begin with a magic ring and 1 ch st, which doesn't count as a st. For example, work 6sc in the ring. Mark the 1st st with a stitch marker. Without closing the round, work the 1st st of the next round directly over the 1st st of the 1st round.

Increase stitch

Whether you're at the edge of or in the middle of a row or round, the principle is the same: work 2 sts in the same st. You can increase by more than one st as well, for example, working 4sc into one st.

Decrease stitch, or crocheting together

Whether you're at the edge of or in the middle of a row or round, the principle is the same: 2 sts will be crocheted together. Where 2 sts were in the row below, the current row will only have 1.

1 To crochet 2 sc together (sc2tog), insert the hook into the st, wrap the yarn, and pull it through. Without finishing the st, insert the hook into the 2nd st, wrap the yarn and pull it through.

You will have 3 loops on the hook.

2 Wrap the yarn and pull through all 3 loops. The stitches are now crocheted together into 1 st.

Changing Colors

The essential feature of changing colors in crochet is that you change the yarn color before you have completed the last st using the old color.

To change colors, work the last st in the old color until 2 loops are left on the hook. Wrap the new yarn color and finish the st with the new color.

Continue working with the new color. Both ends will lie on the wrong side of the work.

With sc, begin with the new color immediately after pulling the yarn through the stitch.

Slip Stitch (slst)

Slip stitches are the smallest stitches. They essentially consist of a single loop.

1 Insert hook into a st, wrap the yarn and pull it through the st.

2 Pull this loop through the loop on the hook without wrapping the yarn.

Half Double Crochet (hdc)

A half double crochet is a little bigger than a sc. It is still compact and creates a dense and robust fabric, but it is more elastic.

1 Wrap the yarn, then insert the hook into the st.

2 Wrap the yarn again and pull through. You will have 3 loops on the hook.

3 Wrap the yarn and pull through all 3 loops on the hook.

4 The hdc is recognizable by its slightly elongated "body" and its short, slanted loop.

Double Crochet (dc)

The simple double crochet is made taller than the sc and the hdc by way of an additional wrap and step.

1 Wrap the yarn, then insert the hook into the st.

2 Wrap the yarn again and pull through. You will have 3 loops on the hook.

3 Wrap the yarn and pull through 2 loops on the hook.

4 Wrap the yarn and pull through the remaining 2 loops on the hook.

5 The dc is recognizable by its long "body" and the diagonal loop in the middle.

Larger stitches (such as tr)

Crochet sts can be increased in the same manner as the dc, simply by adding wraps and steps. The sts get longer with each wrap and step. The treble crochet (tr) is an example.

Treble Crochet (tr)

1 Wrap the yarn twice, then insert the hook into the st.

2 Wrap the yarn and pull through. You will have 4 loops on the hook.

3 Wrap the yarn and pull through the 1st 2 loops on the hook.

4 Wrap the yarn and pull through the next 2 loops on the hook.

5 Wrap the yarn and pull through the last 2 loops on the hook.

6 The tr is recognizable as an even longer st with 2 diagonal loops in the middle.

Double Treble Crochet (dtr)

1 Wrap the yarn three times, then insert the hook into the st. Wrap the yarn and pull through. You will have 5 loops on the hook.

2 In the same manner as the treble crochet, wrap and pull through the 1st 2 sts on the hook until you finish. First you'll have 4 loops . . .

3 . . . then 3 loops . . .

4 . . . and finally 2 loops.

5 Wrap and pull through the last 2 loops on the hook. The dtr has 3 diagonal loops in the middle.

Loop stitch

1 Insert the hook into the st and wrap the yarn underneath the hook. Hold the yarn up with your pointer finger so there are 2 threads, left and right.

2 Catch the left thread with your hook.

3 Pull the thread behind the right thread forward . . .

4 . . . and through the st. You will have 2 loops on the hook.

5 Catch the left thread and pull it through both loops.

6 Let the loop around your finger go— this is your loop st. The loop will be on the wrong side of the work.

Nub stitch

1 Wrap the yarn and insert the hook into the st.

2 Catch the yarn and pull through the st. You will have 3 loops on the hook.

3 Wrap the yarn and pull through the 1st 2 loops. 2 loops are left on the hook.

4 Repeat steps 1–3 4x, always in the same st. You will have 6 loops on the hook.

5 Wrap the yarn and pull through all 6 loops. The finished nub will always be on the wrong side and will not come to the right side until you have worked the next st.

Gary Gecko

... enjoys an active lifestyle

A Guide to the Best
Rock Climbing Spots
in Your Area

BLACK (FB 110*)

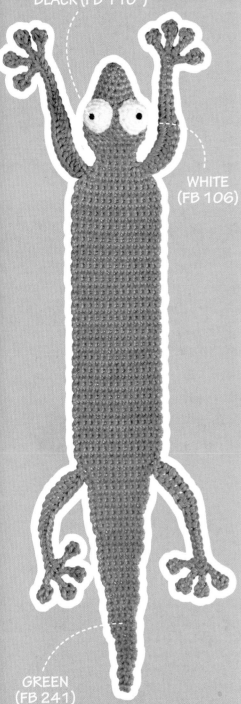

WHITE
(FB 106)

GREEN
(FB 241)

Head

Work the HEAD in Green in a spiral round.

Rnd 1: 6sc in a magic ring (6).

Rnd 2: [2sc in the next st, 2sc] 2x (8).

Rnd 3: [2sc in the next st, 3sc] 2x (10).

Rnd 4: [2sc in the next st, 4sc] 2x (12).

Rnd 5: [2sc in the next st, 5sc] 2x (14).

Rnd 6: [2sc in the next st, 6sc] 2x (16).

Rnd 7: [2sc in the next st, 7sc] 2x (18).

Rnd 8: [2sc in the next st, 8sc] 2x (20).

Rnd 9: [3sc, 2sc in the next st] around (25).

Rnds 10–12: 25sc (25).

Rnd 13: [3sc, sc2tog] around (20).

Rnd 14: [3sc, sc2tog] around (16).

Stuff the HEAD with stuffing.

Rnd 15: Crochet the HEAD together (see p. 10): 7sc (7).

*The FB numbers in parentheses refer to the Schachenmayr yarn colors listed on page 110.

Body

Work the BODY in Green in rows, working along the 7 sts left at the bottom of the HEAD.

Row 1: 6sc (6).

Row 2: 5sc (5)

Row 3: ch1, 5sc (5).

Row 4: ch1, 2sc in the next st, 3sc, 2sc in the next st, crochet the 1st FRONT LEG (see FRONT LEGS on p. 23).

Row 5: 3sc in the next st on BODY, 5sc, 2sc in the next st, crochet the 2nd FRONT LEG.

Row 6: 3sc in the next st on the BODY, 7sc, 2sc in the next st.

Row 7: ch1, 2sc in the next st, 9sc, 2sc in the next st (13).

Rows 8–46: ch1, 13sc (13).

Row 47: ch1, 13sc, crochet the 1st BACK LEG (see BACK LEGS on p. 24).

Row 48: sc2tog on the BODY, 11sc, crochet the 2nd BACK LEG.

Row 49: sc2tog on the BODY, 10sc.

Tail

Work in Green without cutting the yarn.

Row 1: ch1, 10sc (10).

Row 2: ch1, sc2tog, 8sc (9).

Rows 3–5: ch1, 9sc (9).

Row 6: ch1, sc2tog, 7sc (8).

Rows 7–9: ch1, 8sc (8).

Row 10: ch1, sc2tog, 6sc (7).

Rows 11–13: ch1, 7sc (7).

Row 14: ch1, sc2tog, 5sc (6).

Rows 15–17: ch1, 6sc (6).

Row 18: ch1, sc2tog, 4sc (5).

Rows 19–21: ch1, 5sc (5).

Row 22: ch1, 3sc, sc2tog (4).

Rows 23–25: ch1, 4sc (4).

Row 26: ch1, sc2tog, 2sc (3).

Rows 27–29: ch1, 3sc (3).

Row 30: ch1,1sc, sc2tog (2).

Rows 31–33: ch1, 2sc (2).

Row 34: 1sc.

Cut the yarn, leaving a long tail, and pull it through the last st to fasten off.

Front Legs (2X)

Work in Green without cutting the yarn.

Row 1: ch15, [ch6, 1dc in the 3rd st from the hook, 3slst] 4x.

Insert the hook from the left into the last–worked TOE, wrap the yarn and pull through. Do this for all of the TOES. You'll have 5 loops on your hook.

Wrap the yarn and pull through all 5 loops.

Row 2: 5sc, 3hdc, [1dc, 2dc in the next st] 3x.

Back Legs (2X)

Work in Green without cutting the yarn.

Row 1: ch15, [ch6, 1dc in the 3rd st from the hook, 3slst] 4x.

Insert the hook from the left into the last-worked TOE, wrap the yarn and pull through. Do this for all of the TOES. You'll have 5 loops on your hook. Wrap the yarn and pull through all 5 loops.

Row 2: 5sc, 3hdc, 6dc.

Eyes

Work Variation 1 of the EYES (see p. 10).

Finishing

Sew the EYES over the 6th row before the point on the HEAD, 1st apart from each other.

Weave in ends.

Lisa the Book Rat

...likes to spend time in the library

Selections from the
20 Best Books of the Year

SIZE: ABOUT 12 INCHES

WHITE
(FB 106)

BLACK
(FB 110)

STONE
GRAY
(FB 242)

SOFT APRICOT
(FB 263)

Head

Work the HEAD in Soft Apricot in a spiral round.

Rnd 1: 6sc in a magic ring (6).

Rnd 2: [1sc, 2sc in the next st] around (9).

Rnd 3: [1sc, sc2tog] around (6).

Rnd 4: Change color to Stone Gray, [1sc, 2sc in the next st] (9).

Rnd 5: 1sc, 2sc in the next st, [2sc, 2sc in the next st] 2x, 1sc (12).

Rnd 6: [3sc, 2sc in the next st] around (15).

Rnd 7: [6sc, 2sc in the next st] 2x, 1sc (17).

Rnd 8: [7sc, 2sc in the next st] 2x, 1sc (19).

Rnd 9: [8sc, 2sc in the next st] 2x, 1sc (21).

Rnd 10: [9sc, 2sc in the next st] 2x, 1sc (23).

Rnds 11–15: 23sc (23).

Rnd 16: [6sc, sc2tog] 2x, 5sc, sc2tog (20).

Rnd 17: [3sc, sctog] around (16).

Stuff the HEAD with polyester filling.

Rnd 18: Crochet the HEAD together (see p. 10): 7sc (7).

Body

Work the BODY in Stone Gray in rows, working along the 7 sts left at the bottom of the HEAD.

Row 1: ch1, 2sc in the next st, 5sc, 2sc in the next st, (9).

Row 2: ch1, 2sc in the next st, 7sc, 2sc in the next st (11).

Row 3: Crochet the 1st LEG (see LEGS on p. 29), 11sc along the BODY, crochet the 2nd LEG.

Row 4: 11sc along the BODY (11).

27

Row 5: ch1, 2sc in the next st, 9sc, 2sc in the next st (13).

Rows 6–58: ch1, 13sc (13).

Row 59: 12sc (12).

Row 60: 11sc (11).

Row 61: Crochet the 3rd LEG, 11sc along the BODY, crochet the 4th LEG.

Row 62: 11sc along the BODY.

Row 63: 10sc (10).

Row 64: 9sc (9).

Row 65: 4slst. Work the TAIL: change color to Soft Apricot, ch36, 1sc in the 2nd st from the hook, 24sc, 10hdc.

Change color to Stone Gray, 4slst along the BODY (8).

Legs (4X)

Work in Stone Gray without cutting the yarn.

Row 1: ch12, change color to Soft Apricot, [ch6, 1sc, ch4] 4x.

Insert the hook from the left into the last-worked TOE, wrap the yarn and pull through. Do this for all of the TOES. You'll have 4 loops on your hook. Wrap the yarn and pull through all 4 loops.

Row 2: Change color to Stone Gray, 12sc along the ch.

Ears (2X)

Work in Soft Apricot in a spiral round.

Rnd 1: 5sc in a magic ring (5).

Rnd 2: 2sc in every st (10).

Rnd 3: [1sc, 2sc in the next st] around (15).

Rnd 4: Change color to Stone Gray, 1sc, 2sc in the next st, [2sc, 2sc in the next st] 4x, 1sc (20).

Cut the yarn, leaving a long tail, and pull it through the last st to fasten off.

Eyes

Work Variation 1 of the EYES (see p. 10).

Finishing

Sew the EYES over the 6th row on the HEAD, 1 st apart from each other. Sew the EARS 2 rows above the EYES. Weave in ends.

Felicity Sloth

...loves sweet laziness

Explore New Levels
of Relaxation

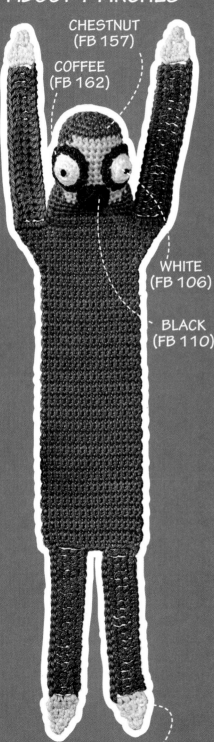

CHESTNUT
(FB 157)

COFFEE
(FB 162)

WHITE
(FB 106)

BLACK
(FB 110)

LINEN (FB 248)

Head

Work the HEAD in Chestnut in a spiral round.

Rnd 1: 6sc in a magic ring (6).

Rnd 2: 2sc in every st (12).

Rnd 3: [1sc, 2sc in the next st] around (18).

Rnd 4: 1sc, 2sc in the next st, [2sc, 2sc in the next st] 5x, 1sc (24).

Rnd 5: [3sc, 2sc in the next st] around (30).

Note: Work Rnds 6–16 only in the front loops.

Rnd 6: 10sc, change color to Linen, 10sc, change color to Chestnut, 10sc (30).

Rnd 7: 9sc, change color to Linen, 12sc, change color to Chestnut, 9sc (30).

Rnds 8–14: 8sc, change color to Linen, 14sc, change color to Chestnut, 8sc (30).

Rnd 15: 9sc, change color to Linen, 12sc, change color to Chestnut, 9sc (30).

Rnd 16: 10sc, change color to Linen, 10sc, change color to Chestnut, 10sc (30).

Rnds 17–19: Working through both front and back loops, 30sc (30).

Stuff the HEAD with polyester filling.

Rnd 20: Crochet the HEAD together (see p. 10): sc14 (14).

Body

Work the BODY in Chestnut in rows, working along the 6 sts left at the bottom of the HEAD.

Row 1: Crochet the 1st ARM (see ARMS on p. 33), 14sc.

Row 2: Crochet the 2nd ARM, 17sc, sc2tog.

Row 3: ch1, 21sc, sc2tog (22).

Row 4: ch1, 20sc, sc2tog (21).

Row 5: ch1, 19sc, sc2tog (20).

Row 6: ch1, 18sc, sc2tog (19).

Row 7: ch1, 17sc, sc2tog (18).

Row 8: ch1, 16sc, sc2tog (17).

Row 9: ch1, 15sc, sc2tog (16).

Rows 10–54: ch1, 16sc (16).

Row 55: ch1, 16sc, crochet 1st LEG (see LEGS on p. 34) (16).

Row 56: 1slst in the 6th st on the BODY, 4slst, crochet 2nd LEG (see LEGS on p. 34), 1slst in the 6th st on the BODY.

Cut the yarn, leaving a long tail, and pull it through the last st to fasten off. Weave in ends.

Arms (2X)

Continue working in Chestnut without cutting the yarn.

Row 1: ch27.

Row 2: 1tr in the 6th st from the hook, 21tr along the ch (22).

Ch1, work 5sc in the last tr.

Legs (2X)

Continue working in Chestnut without cutting the yarn.

Row 1: ch24.

Row 2: 1tr in the 6th st from the hook, 18tr along the ch (19).

Nose

Work the NOSE in Black in a spiral round.

Rnd 1: 6sc in a magic ring (6).

Rnd 2: 2sc in every st (12).

Rnd 3: 12sc (12).

Cut the yarn, leaving a long tail, and pull it through the last st to fasten off.

Paws (4X)

Work the PAWS in Linen in rows.

Row 1: Insert hook through the last tr on the ARM or LEG, grab the yarn and pull through. Ch1.

4sc around the last tr (4).

Rows 2–3: ch1, 4sc (4).

Row 4: 3sc (3).

Row 5: 2sc (2).

Row 6: ch1, sc2tog (1).

Cut the yarn, leaving a long tail, and pull it through the last st to fasten off.

Eyes

Work Variation 3 of the EYES (see p. 11).

Finishing

Center the NOSE on the dividing line between the light and dark parts of the face and sew. Sew the EYES on a slant to the left and right of the NOSE, 3 sts apart, sewing through the dark part of each EYE. Weave in ends.

Franny Flamingo

... loves to travel the world

Dream Destinations for
Globetrotters

SOFT APRICOT
(FB 263)

WHITE
(FB 106)

HOT PINK
(FB 252)

BLACK
(FB 110)

LIGHT PINK
(FB 246)

Head

Work the HEAD in Black in a spiral round.

Rnd 1: 6sc in a magic ring (6).

Rnd 2: [1sc, 2sc in the next st] around (9).

Rnd 3: 9sc (9).

Rnd 4: 1sc, 2sc in the next st, [2sc, 2sc in the next st] 2x, sc (12).

Rnd 5: 12sc (12).

Rnd 6: Change color to Soft Apricot. [3sc, 2sc in the next st] around (15).

Rnd 7: 2sc, 2sc in the next st, [4sc, 2sc in the next st] 2x, 2sc (18).

Rnds 8+9: 18sc (18).

Rnd 10: Change color to White, 18sc (18).

Rnd 11: Change color to Hot Pink and complete this round working only in the front ch. 1sc, 2sc in the next st, [2sc, 2sc in the next st] 5x, sc (24).

Rnd 12: [3sc, 2sc in the next st] around (30).

Rnds 13–17: 30sc (30).

Rnd 18: [3sc, sc2tog] around (24).

Rnd 19: 1sc, sc2tog, [2sc, sc2tog] 5x, 1sc (18).

Rnds 20+21: 18sc (18).

Stuff the HEAD with polyester filling.

Rnd 22: Crochet the HEAD together (see p. 10): 8sc (8).

Body

Work the BODY in Hot Pink in rows, working along the 8 sts left at the bottom of the HEAD.

Row 1: 7sc (7).

Row 2: 6sc (6)

Rows 3–22: ch1, 6sc (6).

Row 23: ch1, 2sc in the next st, 4sc, 2sc in the next st (8).

Row 24: ch1, 2sc in the next st, 6sc, 2sc in the next st (10).

Row 25: ch1, 2sc in the next st, 8sc, 2sc in the next st (12).

Row 26: ch1, 2sc in the next st, 10sc, 2sc in the next st (14).

Feathers

Continue working in Hot Pink in rows without cutting the yarn. Always pick up the yarn from where it was left off. Work the 1st st of each FEATHER in the 3rd st from the hook.

1st Feather: ch4, change color to Black, ch10, 1hdc in the 3rd st from the hook, 2hdc in the next st, [1hdc, 2hdc in the next st] 3x, change color to Hot Pink, 4sc.

Row 1: 14sc along the BODY.

2nd Feather: ch4, change color to Black, ch10, 1hdc in the 3rd st from the hook, 2hdc in the next st, [1hdc, 2hdc in the next st] 3x, change color to Hot Pink, 4sc.

Row 2: 16sc along the BODY, sc2tog.

3rd Feather: Change color to Black, ch9, 2hdc in the 3rd st from the hook, [1hdc, 2hdc in the next st] 3x.

Row 3: change color to Hot Pink, 19sc along the BODY, sc2tog.

4th Feather: change color to Black, ch9, 2hdc in the 3rd st from the hook, [1hdc, 2hdc in the next st] 3x.

Row 4: Change color to Hot Pink, 18sc along the BODY, sc2tog.

5th Feather: Change color to Black, ch8, [1hdc, 2hdc in the next st] 3x.

Row 5: Change color to Hot Pink, 17sc along the BODY, sc2tog.

6th Feather: Change color to Black, ch8, [1hdc, 2hdc in the next st] 3x.

Row 6: Change color to Hot Pink, 16sc along the BODY, sc2tog.

7th Feather: Change color to Black, ch7, 2hdc in the 3rd st from the hook, [1hdc, 2hdc in the next st] 2x.

Row 7: Change color to Hot Pink, 15sc along the BODY, sc2tog.

8th Feather: Change color to Black, ch7, 2hdc in the 3rd st from the hook, [1hdc, 2hdc in the next st] 2x.

Row 8: Change color to Hot Pink, 14sc along the BODY, sc2tog.

9th Feather: Change color to Black, ch6, [1hdc, 2hdc in the next st] 2x.

Row 9: Change color to Hot Pink, 13sc along the BODY, sc2tog.

10th Feather: Change color to Black, ch6, [1hdc, 2hdc in the next st] 2x.

Row 10: Change color to Hot Pink, 12sc along the BODY, sc2tog.

11th Feather: Change color to Black, ch5, 2hdc in the 3rd st from the hook, 1hdc, 2hdc in the next st.

Row 11: Change color to Hot Pink, 11sc along the BODY, sc2tog.

12th Feather: Change color to Black, ch5, 2hdc in the 3rd st from the hook, 1hdc, 2hdc in the next st.

Row 12: Change color to Hot Pink, 12sc along the BODY.

Row 13: ch1, 12sc (12).

Row 14: ch1, sc2tog, 8sc, sc2tog (10).

Row 15: ch1, 10sc (10).

Row 16: ch1, sc2tog, 6sc, sc2tog, (8).

Row 17: ch1, 8sc (8).

Row 18: ch1, 1sc, change color to Light Pink, crochet 1st LEG (see LEGS to the right), change color to Hot Pink, 1sc in the next st on the BODY, 5sc, change color to Light Pink, crochet 2nd LEG (see LEGS to the right), change color to Hot Pink, 1sc in the next st on the BODY.

Cut the yarn, leaving a long tail, and pull it through the last st to fasten off. Weave in ends.

Legs (2X)

Work LEGS in Light Pink. After completing a LEG, pick up the Hot Pink yarn where it was left off, and continue working.

Row 1: ch40.

Row 2: 1tr in the 6th st from the hook, 1tr, 1dc, 1hdc, 14sc, 3dc, 14sc.

Eyes

Work Variation 1 of the EYES (see p. 11).

Finishing

Sew the EYES 2 rows over the White part of the beak on the HEAD, 1 st apart from each other. Weave in all ends.

Paul the Horse

...dreams of becoming a unicorn

Look Within
to Discover the
True You

Head

Work the HEAD in Coffee in a spiral round.

Rnd 1: 6sc in a magic ring (6).

Rnd 2: 2sc in every st (12).

Rnd 3: [3sc, 2sc in the next st] around (15).

Rnd 4: change color to Chestnut, 15sc (15).

Rnd 5: 15sc (15).

Rnd 6: [6sc, 2sc in the next st] 2x, 1sc (17).

Rnd 7: 17sc (17).

Rnd 8: 3sc, 2sc in the next st, 7sc, 2sc in the next st, 5sc (19).

Rnd 9: [3sc, 2sc in the next st] 4x, 2sc, 2sc in the next st (24).

Rnds 10+11: 24sc (24).

Rnd 12: 11sc, 2sc worked through the back loop, 11sc (24).

Rnd 13: 9sc, crochet the 1st EAR (ch4, 1sc in the 2nd st from the hook, 1hdc, 1sc), 1sc in the next st on the HEAD, 4sc in the back loop, 1sc, crochet the 2nd EAR (ch4, 1sc in the 2nd st from the hook, 1hdc, 1sc), 1sc in the next st on the HEAD, 8sc (24).

Rnd 14: 10sc, 4sc in the back loop, 10sc (24).

Rnd 15: 2sc, sc2tog, 2sc, sc2tog, 2sc, 4sc in the back loop, 2sc, sc2tog, 2sc, sc2tog, 2sc (20).

Rnds 16+17: 8sc, 4sc in the back loop, 8sc (20).

Rnd 18: 1sc, sc2tog, 2sc, sc2tog, 1sc, 4sc in the back loop, 1sc, sc2tog, 2sc, sc2tog, 1sc (16).

Rnd 19: 5sc, then stuff the HEAD with stuffing.

Rnd 20: Crochet the HEAD together (see p. 10): 2sc in the next st, 5sc, 2sc in the next st (9).

Body

Work the BODY in Chestnut in rows, working along the 9 sts left at the bottom of the HEAD.

Row 1: ch1, 2sc in the next st, 7sc, 2sc in the next st, crochet the 1st LEG (see LEGS on the right).

Row 2: 1dc+1hdc+2sc in the 1st st on the BODY, 9sc, 2sc in the next st, crochet the 2nd LEG (see LEGS on the right).

Row 3: 1dc+1hdc+1sc in the 1st st on the BODY, 12sc.

Row 4: ch1, 2sc in the next st, 11sc, 2sc in the next st (15).

Rows 5–59: ch1, 15sc (15).

Row 60: ch1, sc2tog, 11sc, sc2tog (13).

Row 61: ch1, 13sc (13).

Row 62: ch1, 1sc, crochet the 3rd LEG (see LEGS on the right), 1sc in the next st on the BODY, 5sc, ch3, 1sc in the same st on the BODY that was last worked, 5sc, crochet the 4th LEG (see LEGS on the right), 1sc in the next st on the BODY.

Cut the yarn, leaving a long tail, and pull it through the last st to fasten off. Weave in ends.

Legs (4X)

Work in Chestnut without cutting the yarn. Always pick up the yarn from where it was left off.

Row 1: ch10, change color to Coffee, ch5.

Row 2: 1dc in the 4th st from the hook, 1dc, change color to Chestnut, 10dc.

Eyes

Work Variation 1 of the EYES (see p. 10).

Finishing

For the MANE, cut 26 pieces of black yarn into 4" strands. Using a yarn needle, pull each strand from back to front (toward the snout) through one of the 26 loops on the HEAD (left from when you worked through the back loop). Pull the strand so its two ends are even and tie it in a knot.

For the TAIL, cut at least 10 strands of black yarn to the same length and pull through a loop between the two back LEGS. Use an extra strand of black yarn to tie these strands into a bundle at the base of the BODY. Tie tightly to fasten.

Sew the EYES to the HEAD beneath the MANE, 1 st apart from each other. Weave in all ends.

44

Elmer the Unicorn

...Paul the Horse's Secret Identity

Head, Body, Eyes

Work the Unicorn in Pink like the Horse (see pp. 41–44), working the HEAD in Pink without changing colors, and working the HOOVES in Mauve.

SIZE: ABOUT 11.5 INCHES

WHITE
(FB 106)

SILVER
(FB 172)

BLACK
(FB 110)

LIGHT PINK
(FB 246)

MAUVE
(FB 399)

RAINBOW COLORS

Horn

Work the HORN in Silver in a spiral round.

Rnd 1: 5sc in a magic ring (5).

Rnds 2–5: 5sc (5).

For the MANE, cut 26 pieces of yarn in Rainbow Colors into 4" strands. Attach as with the Horse, changing color every thread.

For the TAIL, work the same as the Horse but with Rainbow Colors.

Work the EYES the same as the Horse. Weave in ends.

Finishing

Sew the HORN in the middle of the HEAD between the 1st two rows of loops (left from working in the back loop).

Filomena Fox

...is a smarty pants

How to Know It All and
Still Make Friends

SIZE:
ABOUT 11 INCHES

BLACK
(FB 110)

WHITE
(FB 106)

CREAM
(FB 130)

TERRACOTTA
(FB 388)

Head

Work the HEAD in Black in a spiral round.

Rnd 1: 6sc in a magic ring (6).

Rnd 2: [1sc, 2sc in the next st] around (9).

Rnd 3: Change color to Cream, 9sc (9).

Rnd 4: 9sc (9).

Rnd 5: [2sc, 2sc in the next st] around (12).

Rnd 6: Change color to Terracotta, 12sc (12).

Rnd 7: [1sc, 2sc in the next st] around (18).

Rnd 8: [3sc, 2sc in the next st] 4x, 2sc (22).

Rnd 9: 2sc in the next st, 21 sc (23).

Rnd 10: 11sc, 2sc in the next st, 11sc (24).

Rnd 11: 2sc in the next st, 23 sc (25).

Rnds 12–14: 25sc (25).

Rnd 15: [3sc, sc2tog] around (20).

Rnd 16: [3sc, sc2tog] around (20).

Rnd 17: 16sc (16).

Rnd 18: Crochet the HEAD together (see p. 10): 2sc in the next st, 5s, 2sc in the next st (9).

Body

Work the BODY in Terracotta in rows, working along the 9 sts left at the bottom of the HEAD.

Row 1: ch1, 2sc in the next st, 7sc, 2sc in the next st, crochet the 1st LEG (see LEGS instructions on p. 52).

Row 2: 3sc in the next st on the BODY, 10sc, crochet the 2nd LEG.

Row 3: 3sc in the next st on the BODY, 11sc.

Rows 4+5: ch1, 13sc (13).

Row 6: ch1, 2sc in the next st, 11sc, 2sc in the next st (15).

Rows 7–21: ch1, 15sc (15).

Row 22: ch1, sc2tog, 11sc, sc2tog (13).

Row 23: ch1, 13sc (13).

Row 24: ch1, sc2tog, 9sc, sc2tog (11).

Row 25: ch1, 11sc, crochet the 3rd LEG.

Row 26: 1sc in the next st on the BODY, 10sc, crochet the 4th LEG.

Tail

Continue to work in Terracotta in rows.

Row 1: 1slst in the next st on the BODY, 3slst, ch1, 1sc in the 2nd st from the hook, 2sc.

Row 2: ch1, 2sc in the next st, 1sc, 2sc in the next st (5).

Row 3: ch1, 5sc (5).

Row 4: ch1, 2sc in the next st, 3sc, 2sc in the next st (7).

Rows 5+6: ch1, 7sc (7).

Row 7: ch1, 2sc in the next st, 5sc, 2sc in the next st (9).

Rows 8+9: ch1, 9sc (9).

Row 10: ch1, 2sc in the next st, 7sc, 2sc in the next st (11).

Rows 11+12: ch1, 11sc (11).

Row 13: ch1, 2sc in the next st, 9sc, 2sc in the next st (13).

Rows 14–28: ch1, 13sc (13).

Row 29: Change color to Cream, ch1, 13sc (13).

Row 30: ch1, sc2tog, 9sc, sc2tog (11).

Rows 31+32: ch1, 11sc (11).

Row 33: ch1, sc2tog, 7sc, sc2tog (9).

Rows 34+35: ch1, 9sc (9).

Row 36: ch1, sc2tog, 5sc, sc2tog (7).

Rows 37+38: ch1, 7sc (7).

Row 39: ch1, sc2tog, 3sc, sc2tog (5).

Rows 40+41: ch1, 5sc (5).

Row 42: ch1, sc2tog, 1sc, sc2tog (3).

Rows 43+44: ch1, 3sc (3).

Row 45: ch1, sc3tog (1).

Row 46: ch1, 1sc.

Cut the yarn, leaving a long tail, and pull it through the last st to fasten off.

Ears (2X)

Work the EARS in Cream in a spiral round.

Rnd 1: 3sc in a magic ring (3).

Rnd 2: 4sc in every sc (12).

Rnd 3: 2sc, [4sc in the next st, 3sc] 2x, 2sc in the next st, change color to Terracotta, 2sc in the same st as the last 2sc in the next st, 1sc (21).

Rnd 4: 4sc, 4sc in the next st, 7sc.

Rnd 5: ch1 and turn, 4sc, change color to Black, 4sc, 4sc in the next st, 5sc, change color to Terracotta, 3sc, 2sc in the next st.

Rnd 6: sc2tog 5x.

Cut the yarn, leaving a long tail, and pull it through the last st to fasten off.

Legs (4X)

Work in Terracotta without cutting the yarn. Always pick up the yarn from where it was left off.

Row 1: ch5, change color to Black, ch5, [ch4, 1hdc in the 2nd st from hook, 1sc, 1slst] 4x.

Insert the hook from the left into the last-worked TOE, wrap the yarn and pull through. Do this for all of the TOES. You'll have 5 loops on your hook. Wrap the yarn and pull through all 5 loops.

Row 2: 5sc along the Black ch, change color to Terracotta, 5sc along the Terracotta ch.

Eyes

Work Variation 1 of the EYES on p. 10.

Finishing

Sew the EARS two rows over the Cream part of the snout on the HEAD, 1st apart from each other. Sew the EARS 2 rows above the EYES. Weave in ends.

Manuel Mouse

...loves a good cheddar

Cooking With Cheese:
50 Tasty Recipes

SIZE:
ABOUT 13 INCHES

BLACK
(FB 110)

WHITE
(FB 106)

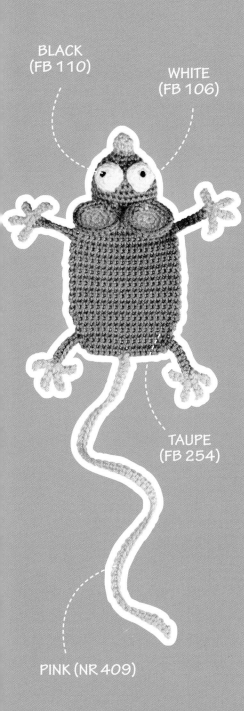

TAUPE
(FB 254)

PINK (NR 409)

Head

Work the HEAD in Pink in a spiral round.

Rnd 1: 6sc in a magic ring (6).

Rnd 2: [1sc, 2sc in the next st] around (9).

Rnd 3: [1sc, sc2tog] around (6).

Rnd 4: Change color to Taupe, [1sc, 2sc in the next st] around (9).

Rnd 5: [2sc, 2sc in the next st] around (12).

Rnd 6: [1sc, 2sc in the next st] around (18).

Rnd 7: 2sc, 2sc in the next st, [2sc, 2sc in the next st] 5x, 1sc (24).

Rnd 8: [3sc, 2sc in the next st] around (30).

Rnds 9–12: 30sc (30).

Rnd 13: [3sc, sc2tog] around (24).

Rnd 14: 24sc (24).

Rnd 15: [2sc, sc2tog] around (18).

Rnd 16: 1sc, 2sc in the next st, [2sc, 2sc in the next st] 5x, 1sc (24).

Rnd 17: [3sc, 2sc in the next st] around (30).

Stuff the HEAD with stuffing.

Rnd 18: Crochet the HEAD together (see p. 10): 2sc in the next st, 12sc, 2sc in the next st (16).

Body

Work the BODY in Taupe in rows, working along the 16 sts left at the bottom of the HEAD.

Row 1: ch1, 2sc in the next st, 14sc, 2sc in the next st, crochet the 1st LEG (see LEGS on p. 56).

Row 2: 2sc in the next st on the BODY; 17sc, crochet the 2nd LEG.

Row 3: 2sc in the next st on the BODY, 17 sc.

Rows 4–15: ch1, 18sc (18).

Row 16: 17sc (17).

Row 17: 16sc, crochet the 3rd LEG.

Row 18: 16sc along the BODY, crochet the 4th LEG.

Row 19: 16sc along the BODY (16).

Row 20: 15sc (15).

Row 21: 1slst, 6sc. Work the TAIL: change color to Pink, ch60, 1sc in the 2nd st from the hook, 58sc. Change color to Taupe and work the rest of Row 21: 1sc in the next st on the BODY, 5sc, 1slst.

Cut the yarn, leaving a long tail, and pull it through the last st to fasten off.

Legs (4X)

Work in Taupe without cutting the yarn. Always pick up the yarn from where it was left off.

Row 1: ch6, change color to Pink, [ch4, 1sc in the 2nd st from the hook, 2slst] 4x.

Insert the hook from the left into the last–worked TOE, wrap the yarn and pull through. Do this for all of the TOES. You'll have 5 loops on your hook. Wrap the yarn and pull through all 5 loops.

Eyes

Work Variation 1 of the EYES
(see p. 10).

Finishing

Sew the EYES 3 rows over the NOSE
on the HEAD, 1st apart from each
other. Sew the EARS 2 rows above the
EYES. Weave in ends.

Ears (2X)

Work the EARS in Pink in
a spiral round.

Rnd 1: 6sc in a magic ring (6).

Rnd 2: 2sc in every st (12).

Rnd 3: [1sc, 2sc in the next st]
around (18).

Rnd 4: Change color to Taupe,
1sc, 2sc in the next st, [2sc, 2sc in
the next st] 5x, 1sc (24).

Cut the yarn, leaving a long tail, and
pull it through the last st to fasten off.

Row 2: Change color to Taupe.
6sc along the ch.

57

Gloria Giraffe

...catches cold easily

A Beginner's Guide
to Scarf Making

SIZE:
ABOUT 12.5 INCHES

BLACK (FB 110)

WHITE (FB 106)

CHESTNUT (FB 157)

GOLD (FB 249)

Head

Work the HEAD in Chestnut in a spiral round.

Rnd 1: 6sc in a magic ring (6).

Rnd 2: 2sc in every st (12).

Rnd 3: [3sc, 2sc in the next st] around (15).

Rnd 4: Change color to Gold, 15sc (15).

Rnd 5: 15sc (15).

Rnd 6: [6sc, 2sc in the next st] 2x, 1sc (17).

Rnd 7: 17sc (17).

Rnd 8: 3sc, 2sc in the next st, 7sc, 2sc in the next st, 5sc (19).

Rnd 9: [3sc, 2sc in the next st] 4x, 2sc, 2sc in the next st (24).

Rnds 10–12: 24sc (24).

Rnd 13: 10sc, crochet the 1st EAR (see EARS on p. 62), 3sc on HEAD, change color to Chestnut, crochet the 1st HORN (see HORNS on p. 62), change color to Gold, 3sc on HEAD, change color to Chestnut, crochet the 2nd HORN, change color to Gold, 3sc on HEAD, crochet 2nd EAR, 5sc on HEAD (24).

Rnds 14+15: 24sc (24).

Rnd 16: 1sc, sc2tog, [2sc, sc2tog] 5x, 1sc (18).

Rnd 17: 18sc (18).

Rnd 18: 17sc, stuff the HEAD with stuffing.

Rnd 19: Crochet the HEAD together (see p. 10): 8sc (8).

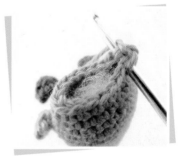

Neck

Work the NECK in Gold in rows, working along the 8 sts left at the bottom of the HEAD.

Row 1: ch1, sc2tog, 4sc, sc2tog (6).

Rows 2–6: ch1, 6sc (6).

From now on, work the SPOT patterns alternately (SPOT 1, SPOT 2, SPOT 1, SPOT 2).

Spot 1

Row 1: ch1, 4sc, change color to Chestnut, 2sc (6).

Row 2: ch1, 3sc, change color to Gold, 2sc (6).

Row 3: ch1, 3sc, change color to Chestnut, 3sc (6).

Row 4: ch1, 3sc, change color to Gold, 3sc (6).

Row 5: ch1, 4sc, change color to Chestnut, 2sc (6).

Rows 6–10: Change color to Gold, ch1, 6sc (6).

Spot 2

Row 1: Change color to Chestnut, ch1, 2sc, change color to Gold, 4sc (6).

Row 2: ch1, 3sc, change color to Chestnut, 3sc (6).

Row 3: ch1, 3sc, change color to Gold, 3sc (6).

Row 4: ch1, 3sc, change color to Chestnut, 3sc (6).

Row 5: ch1, 2sc, change color to Gold, 4sc (6).

Rows 6–10: ch1, 6sc (6).

Body

Continue to work in Gold in rows.

Row 1: ch1, 2sc in the next st, 4sc, 2sc in the next st (8).

Row 2: ch1, 8sc (8).

Row 3: ch1, 2sc in the next st, 6sc, 2sc in the next st (10).

Row 4: ch1, 10sc (10).

Row 5: ch1, 2sc in the next st, 8sc, 2sc in the next st (12).

Row 6: ch1, 10sc, crochet 1st LEG (see LEGS on p. 63).

Row 7: 1hdc+2sc in the next st on BODY, 13sc, crochet 2nd LEG.

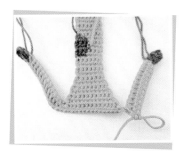

Row 8: 1hdc+2sc in the next st on BODY, 14sc.

Row 9: ch1, 3sc, change color to Chestnut, 4sc, change color to Gold, 9sc (16).

Row 10: ch1, 8sc, change color to Chestnut, 6sc, change color to Gold, 2sc (16).

Row 11: ch1, 2sc, change color to Chestnut, 6sc, change color to Gold, 8sc (16).

Row 12: ch1, 8sc, change color to Chestnut, 6sc, change color to Gold, 2sc (16).

Row 13: ch1, 2sc, change color to Chestnut, 6sc, change color to Gold, 8sc (16).

Row 14: ch1, 9sc, change color to Chestnut, 4sc, change color to Gold, 3sc (16).

Rows 15–17: ch1, 16sc (16).

Row 18: ch1, 3sc, change color to Chestnut, 4sc, change color to Gold, 9sc (16).

Row 19: ch1, 8sc, change color to Chestnut, 6sc, change color to Gold, 2sc (16).

Row 20: ch1, 2sc, change color to Chestnut, 6sc, change color to Gold, 8sc (16).

Row 21: ch1, 8sc, change color to Chestnut, 6sc, change color to Gold, 2sc (16).

Row 22: ch1, 2sc, change color to Chestnut, 6sc, change color to Gold, 8sc (16).

Row 23: ch1, 9sc, change color to Chestnut, 4sc, change color to Gold, 3sc (16).

Row 24: ch1, 16sc (16).

Row 25: ch1, sc2tog, 12sc, sc2tog (14).

Row 26: ch1, 14sc (14).

Row 27: ch1, 1sc, crochet 3rd LEG, 1sc in the next st on the BODY, 4sc. Work the TAIL: ch9, 1sc in the 2nd st from hook, 7sc. 1sc in the next st on the BODY, 5sc, crochet 4th LEG, 1sc in the next st on the BODY.

Cut the yarn, leaving a long tail, and pull it through the last st to fasten off.

Ears (2X)

Work in Gold without cutting the yarn.

Row 1: ch6.

Row 2: 1sc in the 2nd st from the hook, 1hdc, 2dc, 1slst.

Horns (2X)

Work in Chestnut without cutting the yarn.

Row 1: ch7.

Row 2: 2dc in the 4th st from the hook, 3slst.

Legs (4X)

Work in Gold without cutting the yarn. Always pick up the yarn from where it was left off.

Row 1: ch12, change color to Chestnut, ch5.

Row 2: 1dc in the 4th st from the hook, 1dc, change color to Gold, 12dc.

Eyes

Work Variation 1 of the EYES (see p. 10).

Finishing

Sew the EYES 3 rows below the EARS and HORNS on the HEAD, 1st apart from each other. For the tuft on the TAIL, take a few strands of Chestnut yarn and knot them through the last st on the TAIL. Weave in ends.

Harry Hound

... loves people

People Whisperer:
The Incredible Story of the Dog
That Trained Humans

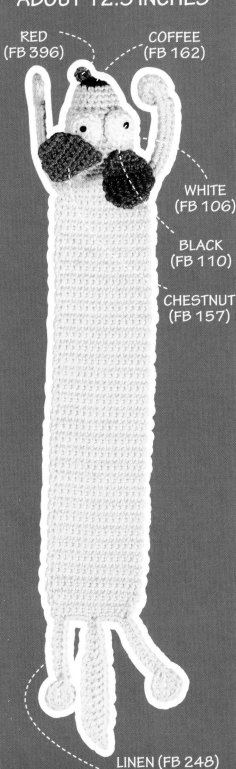

RED
(FB 396)

COFFEE
(FB 162)

WHITE
(FB 106)

BLACK
(FB 110)

CHESTNUT
(FB 157)

LINEN (FB 248)

Head

Work the HEAD in Coffee in a spiral round.

Rnd 1: 6sc in a magic ring (6).

Rnd 2: 2sc in every st (12).

Rnd 3: Change color to Linen, [3sc, 2sc in the next st] around (15).

Rnd 4: 2sc, 2sc in the next st, [4sc, 2sc in the next st] 2x, 2sc (18).

Rnds 5+6: 18sc (18).

Rnd 7: Work this round only through the front loops. 1sc, 2sc in the next st, [2sc, 2sc in the next st] 5x, 1sc (24).

Rnd 8: [5sc, 2sc in the next st] around (28).

Rnds 9–12: 28sc (28).

Rnd 13: 5sc, sc2tog (24).

Rnd 14: 24sc (24).

Rnd 15: 1sc, sc2tog [2sc, sc2tog] 5x, 1sc (18).

Rnds 16+17: 18sc (18).

Stuff the HEAD with polyester filling.

Rnd 18: Crochet the HEAD together (see p. 10): 2sc in the next st, 6sc, 2sc in the next st (10).

Body

Work the BODY in Linen in rows, working along the 10 sts left at the bottom of the HEAD.

Row 1: ch1, 2sc in the next st, 8sc, 2sc in the next st, crochet 1st FRONT LEG (see FRONT LEGS on p. 67).

Row 2: 1hdc+2sc in the 1st st on BODY, 11sc along the BODY, crochet 2nd FRONT LEG.

Row 3: 1hdc+2sc in the 1st st on BODY, 12sc.

Rows 4–64: ch1, 14sc (14).

Row 65: ch1, sc2tog, 10sc, sc2tog (12).

Row 66: ch1, 12sc (12).

Row 67: ch1, 1sc, crochet 1st BACK LEG (see BACK LEGS on p. 67), 1sc in the next st on BODY, 4sc.

Work the TAIL: ch18, sc in the 2nd st from the hook, 1hdc, 1dc, 9tr, 3dc, 2hdc. 2sc in the next st on the BODY, 4sc, crochet the 2nd BACK LEG, 1sc in the next st on the BODY.

Cut the yarn, leaving a long tail, and pull it through the last st to fasten off.

Front Legs (2X)

Work in Linen without cutting the yarn.

Row 1: ch18.

Row 2: 10hdc in the 3rd st from the hook, 1slst in the 1st hdc to close the circle. 11hdc along the ch, doubling every 2nd hdc (the number of hdc on the ch can vary, depending on how much of the ch the circle "absorbed").

Back Legs (2X)

Work in Linen without cutting the yarn.

Row 1: ch15.

Row 2: 10hdc in the 3rd st from the hook, 1slst in the 1st hdc to close the circle. 11hdc along the ch, doubling every 2nd hdc (the number of hdc on the ch can vary, depending on how much of the ch the circle "absorbed").

Ears (2X)

Work in Chestnut in rows. Leave a long tail at the beginning for easy sewing later.

Row 1: ch4.

Row 2: 1sc in the 2nd st from the hook, 2sc (3).

Row 3: ch1, 2sc in the next st, 1sc, 2sc in the next st (5).

Row 4: ch1, 2sc in the next st, 3sc, 2sc in the next st (7).

Rows 5–9: 7sc (7).

Row 10: ch1, sc2tog, 3sc, sc2tog (5).

Row 11: ch1, 5sc (5).

Row 12: ch1, sc2tog, 1sc, sc2tog (3).

Cut the yarn, leaving a long tail, and pull it through the last st to fasten off.

Tongue

Work the TONGUE in Red in rows.

Row 1: ch4.

Row 2: 1hdc in the 3rd st from the hook, 1hdc (2).

Cut the yarn, leaving a long tail, and pull it through the last st to fasten off.

Eyes

Work Variation 2 of the EYES (see p. 11).

Finishing

Using a yarn needle, thread both ends of the TONGUE through the underside of the Coffee-colored SNOUT and sew on the border between the Coffee and Linen. Sew the EYES onto the HEAD on the row where you worked through the front loops, 1st apart from each other. Sew the EARS 1 row over the EYES, 1st apart.

Weave in ends.

Karl Cat

...prefers to be alone

How to Find Yourself in Those Quiet Moments of Solitude

RASPBERRY
(FB 256)

GARNET
(FB 413)

STONE
GRAY
(FB 242)

BLACK
(FB 110)

WHITE
(FB 106)

Head

Work the HEAD in Black in a spiral round.

Rnd 1: 7sc in a magic ring (7).

Rnd 2: [1sc, 2sc in the next st] 3x, 1sc (10).

Rnd 3: [2sc in the next st, 2sc] 3x, 2sc in the next st (14).

Rnd 4: [2sc in the next st, 3sc] 3x, 2sc in the next st, 1sc (18).

Rnd 5: [2sc in the next st, 4sc] 3x, 2sc in the next st, 2sc (22).

Rnd 6: [2sc in the next st, 5sc] 3x, 2sc in the next st, 3sc (26).

Rnd 7: [2sc in the next st, 6sc] 3x, 2sc in the next st, 4sc (30).

Rnds 8–12: 30sc (30).

Rnd 13: [3sc, sc2tog] around (24).

Rnd 14: 1sc sc2tog [2sc, sc2tog] 4x, 1sc (18).

Rnd 15: 18sc (18).

Stuff the HEAD with polyester filling.

Rnd 16: Crochet the HEAD together (see p. 10): 2sc in the next st, 6sc, 2sc in the next st (10).

Body

Work the BODY in Black in rows, working along the 10 sts left at the bottom of the HEAD.

Row 1: ch1, 2sc in the next st, 8sc, 2sc in the next st, crochet the 1st FRONT LEG (see FRONT LEGS on right).

Row 2: 1dc+1hdc+1sc in the 2nd st on BODY, 11sc, crochet the 2nd FRONT LEG.

Row 3: 1dc+1hdc+1sc in the 1st st on BODY, 13sc.

Rows 4–29: ch1, 16sc (16).

Row 30: ch1, sc2tog, 12sc, sc2tog (14).

Row 31: ch1, 14sc (14).

Row 32: ch1, 1sch, crochet the 1st BACK LEG (see BACK LEGS on p. 74), 1sc in the next st on BODY, 5sc, crochet the TAIL (see TAIL on p. 74), 1sc in the next st on BODY, 5sc, crochet the 2nd BACK LEG, 2sc in the next st on the BODY.

Cut the yarn, leaving a long tail, and pull it through the last st to fasten off.

Front Legs (2X)

Work in Black without cutting the yarn. Always pick up the yarn from where it was left off.

Row 1: ch10, change color to White, ch7.

Row 2: 1dc in the 4th st from the hook, 2dc in the next st, 1dc, 2dc in the next st, change color to Black, [1dc, 2dc in the next st] 5x.

Back Legs (2X)

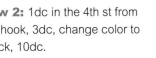

Work in Black without cutting the yarn. Always pick up the yarn from where it was left off.

Row 1: ch10, change color to White, ch7.

Row 2: 1dc in the 4th st from the hook, 3dc, change color to Black, 10dc.

Tail

Work in Black without cutting the yarn. Always pick up the yarn from where it was left off.

Row 1: ch30, change color to White, ch18.

Row 2: 1dc in the 4th st from hook, 14tr, change color to Black, 27tr, 3dc.

Ears (2X)

Work the EARS in Stone Gray in a spiral round.

Rnd 1: 3sc in a magic ring (3).

Rnd 2: 4sc in the next st (12).

Rnd 3: 2sc, [4sc in each st, 3sc] 2x, 2sc in the next st, change color to Black, in the same st last worked, 1sc (21).

Rnd 4: 6sc, [4sc in the next st, 6sc] 2x, 2sc in the next st (28).

Cut the yarn, leaving a long tail, and pull it through the last st to fasten off.

Yarn Ball

Work the YARN BALL in Garnet in a spiral round.

Rnd 1: 6sc in a magic ring (6).

Rnd 2: 2sc in every st (12).

Rnd 3: [1sc, 2sc in the next st] around (18).

Rnds 4–7: 18sc (18).

Rnd 8: [1sc, sc2tog] around (12).

Rnd 9: Stuff the YARN BALL with stuffing. [sc2tog] 6x (6).

Cut the yarn, leaving a long tail, and pull it through all sts to fasten off. Sew strands of Raspberry through to the YARN BALL to make it look more textured.

Eyes

Work Variation 1 of the EYES (see p. 10).

(see p. 10).

Finishing

Sew the EYES 6 rows above the NOSE on the HEAD, 1st apart from each other. Sew the EARS to the HEAD 1 row above the EYES. Sew the YARN BALL with a White strand to one of the White PAWS. Weave in ends.

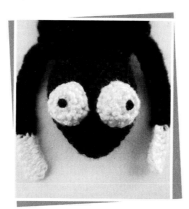

Luis Lion

... is a peace-loving eco-warrior

Even a Vegan Can Be King of the Jungle

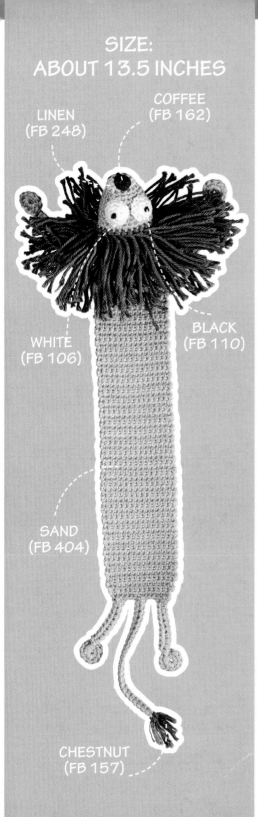

SIZE:
ABOUT 13.5 INCHES

LINEN
(FB 248)

COFFEE
(FB 162)

WHITE
(FB 106)

BLACK
(FB 110)

SAND
(FB 404)

CHESTNUT
(FB 157)

Head

Work the HEAD in Linen in a spiral round.

Rnd 1: 6sc in a magic ring (6).

Rnd 2: 2sc in every st (12).

Rnd 3: [3sc, 2sc in the next st] around (15).

Rnd 4: 15sc (15).

Rnd 5: Change color to Sand, work this round only through the front loops. 2sc, 2sc in the next st, [4sc, 2sc in the next st] 2x, 2sc (18).

Rnd 6: [3sc, 2sc in the next st] 4x, 2sc (22).

Rnd 7: 2sc, 2sc in the next st, [4sc, 2sc in the next st] 3x, 4sc (26).

Rnds 8–12: 26sc (26).

Rnd 13: Change color to Chestnut, ch1, turn and continue to crochet in the opposite direction. 26 loop sts (see p. 18) (26).

Rnds 14–17: 26 loop-sts (26).

Rnd 18: 5 loop-sts, sc2tog, 4 loop-sts, sc2tog, 5 loop-sts, sc2tog, 4 loop-sts, sc2tog (22).

Rnd 19: ch1, turn and continue to crochet in the opposite direction. 22sc, 1slst in the 1st st in the rnd to close the rnd.

Stuff the HEAD with polyester filling.

Rnd 20: Crochet the HEAD together (see p. 10): 2sc in the next st, 8sc, 2sc in the next st (12).

Body

Work the BODY in Sand in rows, working along the 12 sts left at the bottom of the HEAD.

Row 1: ch1, 2sc in the next st, 10sc, 2sc in the next st, crochet 1st FRONT LEG (see FRONT LEGS on p. 79).

Row 2: 1hdc+1sc in the 1st st on the BODY, 13sc along the BODY, crochet 2nd FRONT LEG.

Row 3: 1hdc+1sc in the 1st st on the BODY, 14sc along the BODY.

Row 4: ch1, 16sc (16).

Row 5: ch1, sc2tog, 14sc (15).

Row 6: ch1, sc2tog, 13sc (14).

Row 7–61: ch1, 14sc (14).

Row 62: ch1, sc2tog, 10sc, sc2tog (12).

Row 63: ch1, 12sc (12).

Row 64: ch1, 1sc, crochet 1st BACK LEG (see BACK LEGS on p. 79), 1sc in the next st on BODY, 5slst.

Work the TAIL: ch25, 2hdc in the 3rd st from hook, 22hdc. 4slst along the BODY, 1sc, crochet 2nd BACK LEG.

Cut the yarn, leaving a long tail, and pull it through the last st to fasten off.

Front Legs (2X)

Work in Sand without cutting the yarn.

Row 1: ch20.

Row 2: 10hdc in the 3rd st from hook, 1slst in the 1st hdc to close the circle. 13hdc along the ch (the number of hdc can vary, depending on how much of the ch is "absorbed" by the circle.)

Back Legs (2X)

Work in Sand without cutting the yarn.

Row 1: ch15.

Row 2: 10hdc in the 3rd st from hook, 1slst in the 1st hdc to close the circle. 9hdc along the ch (the number of hdc can vary, depending on how much of the ch is "absorbed" by the circle.)

Eyes

Work Variation 1 of the EYES
(see p. 10).

Finishing

For the MANE, cut the loop sts open.
Sew the EYES 1 row below the MANE,
1st apart from each other. With a
strand of Coffee, embroider a dark
NOSE and MOUTH on the Linen
snout. For the TAIL, cut a few strands
of Chestnut, knot them to the end
of the TAIL, and unravel the strands.
Weave in ends.

Freddy Frog

... is a medal-winning long jumper

History's Greatest Olympic Amphibians

WHITE
(FB 106)

RED
(FB 396)

BLACK
(FB 110)

KHAKI
(FB 212)

Head

Work the HEAD in Khaki in a spiral round.

Rnd 1: 6sc in a magic ring (6).

Rnd 2: 2sc in every st (12).

Rnd 3: [1sc, 2sc in the next st] around (18).

Rnd 4: 1sc 2sc in the next st, [2sc, 2sc in the next st] 5x, sc (24).

Rnd 5: [3sc, 2sc in the next st] around (30).

Rnds 6–9: 30sc (30).

Rnd 10: 1sc, ch15, insert hook through the 16th st on HEAD, counted from the beginning of the ch along the HEAD, being careful not to twist the ch, 14sc (30).

Rnds 11+12: 30sc (30).

Rnd 13: [3sc, sc2tog] around (24).

Rnd 14: [2sc, sc2tog] around (18).

Rnds 15+16: 18sc (18).

Rnd 17: 3sc (3).

Rnd 18: Crochet the HEAD together (see p. 10): 2sc in the next st, 6sc, 2sc in the next st (10).

Mouth

Work the MOUTH in Black in a spiral round.

Rnd 1: 6sc in a magic ring (6).

Rnd 2: 2sc in every st (12).

Rnd 3: [1sc, 2sc in the next st] around (18).

Rnd 4: 1sc, 2sc in the next st, [2sc, 2sc in the next st] 5x, sc (24).

Rnd 5: [3sc, 2sc in the next st] around (30).

Tongue

Work the TONGUE in Red in rows.

Row 1: ch30.

Row 2: 1dc in the 4th st from hook, 1dc, 1hdc, 24sc (27).

Cut the yarn, leaving a long tail, and pull it through the last st to fasten off. Thread one end through a yarn needle and pull it through the middle of the MOUTH. Pull the other end through a st next to the middle and tie the two ends together. Trim the yarn.

Stuff the top and bottom halves of the HEAD with polyester filling and fit the MOUTH inside, between the top and bottom lips of the HEAD. Sew through both loops of the MOUTH sts and only the back loop of the HEAD sts.

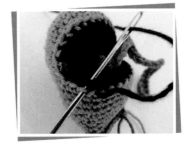

Body

Work the BODY in Khaki in rows, working along the 10 sts left at the bottom of the HEAD.

Row 1: ch1, 2sc in the next st, 8sc, 2sc in the next st (12).

Row 2: ch1, 2sc in the next st, 10sc, 2sc in the next st, crochet 1st FRONT LEG (see FRONT LEGS on right) (14).

Row 3: 3sc in the 1st st on BODY, 13sc, crochet 2nd FRONT LEG.

Row 4: 3sc in the 1st st on BODY, 13sc.

Rows 5–30: ch1, 14sc (14).

Row 31: 11sc, sc2tog (12).

Row 32: ch1, 12sc (12).

Row 33: ch1, 1sc, crochet 2st BACK LEG (see BACK LEGS on p. 85), 1sc in the next st on BODY, 9sc, crochet 2nd BACK LEG, 1sc in the next st on BODY.

Front Legs (2X)

Work in Khaki without cutting the yarn.

Row 1: ch21, 1dc in the 4th st from hook, 3slst, [ch7, 1dc in the th st from hook, 3slst] 3x.

Insert the hook from the left into the last-worked TOE, wrap the yarn and pull through. Do this for all of the TOES. You'll have 5 loops on your hook. Wrap the yarn and pull through all 5 loops.

Work Variation 2 of the EYES (see p. 11).

Row 2: 14sc along the starting ch.

Work the TOES as with the FRONT LEGS. At the end, you'll have 6 loops on the hook instead of 5. Wrap the yarn and pull through all 6 loops.

Finishing

Sew the EYES 1 or 2 rows above the top lip on the HEAD, 1 st apart from each other. Weave in ends.

Back Legs (2X)

Work in Khaki without cutting the yarn.

Row 1: ch45, 1hdc in the 4th st from hook, 3slst, [ch7, 1dc in the 4th st from hook, 3slst] 3x.

Row 2: 38sc along the starting ch.

Selma Snake

... has spiraling stripes

Feel at Home in your Body
Through Self-Affirmation

SIZE: ABOUT 12.5 INCHES

RED (FB 396)

GOLD (FB 249)

SILVER (FB 172)

BLACK (FB 110)

PEACOCK BLUE (FB 146)

Lower Jaw

Work the LOWER JAW in Peacock Blue in a spiral round.

Rnd 1: 6sc in a magic ring (6).

Rnd 2: 2sc in every st (12).

Rnd 3: 2sc in the next st, 11sc (13).

Rnd 4: 2sc in the next st, 12sc (14).

Rnd 5: [6sc, 2sc in the next st] around (16).

Rnds 6+7: 16sc (16).

Rnd 8: [3sc, 2sc in the next st] around (20).

Rnd 9: [3sc, 2sc in the next st] around (25).

Rnds 10–13: 25sc (25).

Rnd 14: 2sc in the next st, 24sc (26).

Rnd 15: Crochet the LOWER JAW together (see p. 10): [sc2tog] around (6).

Row 16: ch1, 2sc in the next st, 4sc, 2sc in the next st (8).

Cut the yarn, leaving a long tail, and pull it through the last st to fasten off.

Upper Jaw

Work the UPPER JAW in Peacock Blue in a spiral round.

Rnd 1: 6sc in a magic ring (6).

Rnd 2: 2sc in every st (12).

Rnd 3: Work this round in the back loop. 2sc in the next st, 11sc (13).

Rnds 4–15: Work the same as the LOWER JAW (p. 87) without cutting the yarn at the end.

Tongue

Work the TONGUE in Red in rows.

Row 1: ch26, [ch5, slst in the 2nd st from hook, 3slst] 2x.

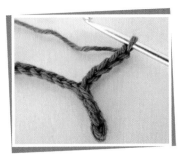

Row 2: 10slst, 16sc.

Cut the yarn, leaving a long tail, and pull it through the last st to fasten off.

Continue working the UPPER JAW in Peacock Blue. Lay the UPPER and LOWER JAWS next to each other, so that the thread from the TOP JAW lies on the right side.

Crochet the UPPER and LOWER JAWS together: insert the hook through the 1st st on both the UPPER and LOWER JAWS. Wrap the yarn and pull through both sts, 1sc.

Work the next 2 st–pairs in the same way (3).

Crochet the TONGUE. Insert the hook as before, placing the TONGUE between the UPPER and LOWER JAWS and inserting the hook through all 3 sts. Wrap the yarn and pull through all 3 sts, 1sc.

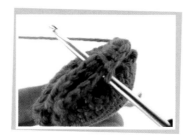

Do this once more so that the TONGUE is snugly attached between the two JAWS.

Work the next 3 st–pairs in the same way as before. The UPPER JAW, LOWER JAW, and TONGUE should now be crocheted together with 8 sts.

Row 1: ch1, 8sc (8).

Body

Work the BODY in Peacock Blue in rows, working along the 8 sts left at the bottom of the HEAD. Alternate between the two following patterns:

Pattern 1: ch1, 2sc, 2hdc, 2dc, 2tr (8).

Pattern 2: ch4, 2tr, 2dc, 2hdc, 2sc (8).

Row 1: Pattern 1.

Row 2: Change color to Black, pattern 2.

Row 3: Change color to Silver, pattern 1.

Row 4: Pattern 1.

Row 5: Change color to Black, pattern 2.

Row 6: Change color to Peacock Blue, pattern 1.

Row 7: Pattern 2.

Row 8: Pattern 1.

Row 9: Pattern 2.

Row 10: Change color to Black, pattern 2.

Row 11: Change color to Silver, pattern 1.

Row 12: Pattern 2.

Row 13: Change color to Black, pattern 1.

Row 14: Change color to Peacock Blue, pattern 2.

Rows 15+16: Pattern 1.

Row 17: Pattern 2.

Row 18: Change color to Black, pattern 1.

Row 19: Change color to Silver, pattern 2.

Row 20: Pattern 1.

Row 21: Change color to Black, pattern 2.

Row 22: Change color to Peacock Blue, pattern 2.

Row 23: Pattern 1.

Row 24: Pattern 2.

Row 25: Pattern 1.

Row 26: Change color to Black, pattern 2.

Row 27: Change color to Silver, pattern 1.

Row 28: Pattern 1.

Row 29: Change color to Black, pattern 2.

Row 30: Change color to Peacock Blue, pattern 1.

Row 31: Pattern 2.

Row 32: Pattern 1.

Row 33: Pattern 2.

Now, stop working patterns 1+2 and work normally.

Row 34: Change color to Black, ch4, 2tr, 2dc, 2hdc, sc2tog (7).

Row 35: Change color to Silver, ch1, 2sc, 2hdc, 2dc, 1tr (7).

Row 36: ch4, 1tr, 2dc, 2hdc, sc2tog (6).

Row 37: Change color to Black, ch1, 2sc, 2hdc, 2dc (6).

Row 38: Change color to Peacock Blue, ch3, 2dc, 2hdc, sc2tog (5).

Row 39: ch1, 2sc, 2hdc, 1dc (5).

Row 40: ch1, sc2tog, 2hdc, 1dc (4).

Row 41: ch2, 2hdc, 2sc (4).

Rows 42–44: ch1, 4sc (4).

Row 45: 3sc (3).

Rows 46+47: ch1, 3sc (3).

Row 48: 2sc (2).

Rows 49+50: ch1, 2sc (2).

Row 51: 1sc (1).

Cut the yarn, leaving a long tail, and pull it through the last st to fasten off.

Eyes

Work the EYES in Gold in Variation 1 (see p .10).

Finishing

Sew the EYES 2 rows before the THROAT (the rnd where the JAWS were crocheted together), 1 st apart from each other. With a strand of Black yarn, sew 2 long pupils on the EYES. Weave in ends.

Daniel Dragon

...wants to be a firefighter

17 Steps to Passing
the Firefighter's Exam

SIZE:
ABOUT 14 INCHES

BLACK
(FB 110)

WHITE
(FB 106)

STONE
GRAY
(FB 242)

WINE
(FB 192)

Head

Work the HEAD in Wine in a spiral round.

Rnd 1: 6sc in a magic ring (6).

Rnd 2: 2sc in every st (12).

Rnd 3: [3sc, 2sc in the next st] around (15).

Rnd 4: 6sc, ch1, 1hdc in the 2nd st from hook, 1sc on HEAD, 2sc, ch2, 1hdc in the 2nd st from hook, 1sc on HEAD, 5sc (15).

Rnd 5: 5sc, 1sc over the NOSTRIL, 3sc, 1sc over the NOSTRIL, 5sc (15).

Rnd 6: 15sc (15).

Rnd 7: 2sc, 2sc in the next st, [4sc, 2sc in the next st] 2x, 2sc (18).

Rnd 8: [5sc, 2sc in the next st] (21).

Rnd 9: 3sc, 2sc in the next st, [6sc, 2sc in the next st] 2x, 3sc (24).

Rnd 10: [7sc, 2sc in the next st] (27).

Rnd 11: 4sc, 2sc in the next st, [8sc, 2sc in the next st] 2x, 4sc (30).

Rnds 12+13: 30sc (30).

Rnd 14: 10sc, crochet 1st EAR (ch4, 1dc in the 3rd st from hook, 1hdc) 1sc in the next st on HEAD, 14sc, crochet 2nd EAR (see 1st EAR), 1sc in the next st on HEAD, 4sc (30).

Rnd 15: 10sc, 1sc over the 1st EAR, 14sc, 1sc over the 2nd EAR, 4sc (30).

Rnd 16: 30 sc (30).

Rnd 17: [3sc, sc2tog] around (24).

Rnd 18: 1sc, sc2tog, [2sc, sc2tog] 5x, 1sc (18).

Rnd 19: 18sc (18).

Rnd 20: 17sc.

Stuff the HEAD with polyester filling.

Rnd 21: Crochet the HEAD together (see p. 10): 8sc (8).

Body

Work the BODY in Wine in rows, working along the 8 sts left at the bottom of the HEAD.

Row 1: ch1, 8sc, crochet 1st WING (see WINGS on p. 96) (8).

Row 2: 1sc in the next st on BODY, 7sc along the BODY, crochet 2nd WING (8).

Row 3: 1sc in the next st on BODY, 7sc along BODY, 1sc in the next st on WING (9).

Row 4: ch1, 9sc along BODY, 1sc in the next st on WING (10).

Row 5: ch1, 10sc along BODY, 1sc in the next st on WING (11).

Row 6: ch1, 11sc along BODY, 1sc in the next st on WING (12).

Row 7: ch1, 12sc along BODY, 2sc in the next st on WING (14).

Row 8: ch1, 14sc along BODY, 2sc in the next st on WING (16).

Rows 9–28: ch1, 16sc (16).

Row 29: ch1, sc2tog, 12sc, sc2tog (14).

Row 30: 1sc, 14sc (14).

Row 31: ch1, 1sc, crochet 1st LEG (see LEGS on p. 97), 1sc in the next st on BODY, 12sc.

Row 32: ch1, 1sc, crochet 2nd LEG, 1sc in the next st on BODY, 1slst, ch1, 1sc in the 2nd st from hook, 7sc.

Rows 33–42: ch1, 8sc (8).

Row 43: ch1, sc2tog, 4sc, sc2tog (6).

Rows 44–64: ch1, 6sc (6).

Row 65: ch1, sc2tog, 2sc, sc2tog (4).

Rows 66–95: ch1, 4sc (4).

Tail Point

Work in rows in Wine.

Row 1: ch5.

Row 2: 1sc in the 2nd st from hook, 3sc, 4sc along TAIL, ch5.

Row 3: 1sc in the 2nd st from hook, 3sc, 8sc along TAIL.

Work the following rows without a beginning ch.

Row 4: 11sc (11).

Row 5: 10sc (10).

Row 6: 9sc (9).

Row 7: 8sc (8).

Row 8: 7sc (7).

Row 9: 6sc (6).

Row 10: 5sc (5).

Row 11: 4sc (4).

Row 12: 3sc (3).

Row 13: 2sc (2).

Row 14: 1sc (1).

Cut the yarn, leaving a long tail, and pull it through the last st to fasten off.

Wings (2X)

Work in Wine without cutting the yarn.

Row 1: ch24.

Row 2: 1sc in the 2nd st from hook, 14sc, 2hdc, 2dc, 4tr (23). 5sc around the last tr.

Legs (2X)

Work in Wine without cutting the yarn.

Row 1: ch8, [ch4, 1sc in the 3nd st from hook, 2sc] 3x.

Insert the hook from the left into the last-worked TOE, wrap the yarn and pull through. Do this for all of the TOES. You'll have 4 loops on your hook. Wrap the yarn and pull through all 4 loops.

Row 2: 8sc along the beginning ch.

Inner Wing

Work in Stone Gray in rows.

Row 1: Insert hook through the last tr, which is at the BODY edge. Pull the yarn through so you have 1 loop on your hook. Ch1.

1sc in the same st as this ch.

20sc along the WING (21).

Row 2: ch1, 9sc, skip 3, 9sc (18).

Row 3: ch1, sc2tog, 6sc, skip 1, 7sc, sc2tog (15).

Row 4: ch1, sc2tog, 5sc, skip 1, 5sc, sc2tog (12).

Row 5: ch1, sc2tog, 3sc, skip 1, 4sc, sc2tog (9).

Row 6: ch1, 1sc, [skip 1, 1sc] 4x, 1sc (5).

Row 7: ch1, 1sc, [skip 1, 1sc] 2x, 1sc (3).

Row 8: Turn, sc2tog (1).

Cut the yarn, leaving a long tail, and pull it through the last st to fasten off.

Ridge

Work in Black in rows.

Row 1: ch6.

Row 2: 1sc in the 2nd st from hook, ch1, 1dc in the next st on the beginning ch, ch2, 1slst in the same st as the dc, 1slst, 1sc, ch1, 1sc in the next st on the beginning ch, ch2, 1slst in the same st as the dc.

Cut the yarn, leaving a long tail, and pull it through the last st to fasten off.

Eyes

Work Variation 1 of the EYES
(see p. 10).

Finishing

Sew the EYES 2 rows above the
NOSTRILS, 1st apart from each
other. Sew the RIDGE just above and
between the EYES. Weave in ends.

Sharon Sheep

...crochets sweaters for her friends

The Ultimate Crochet Guidebook

WHITE
(FB 106)

BLACK
(FB 110)

Head

Work the HEAD in Stone Gray in a spiral round.

Rnd 1: 6sc in a magic ring (6).

Rnd 2: 2sc in every st (12).

Rnd 3: [3sc, 2sc in the next st] around (15).

Rnd 4: 2sc, 2sc in the next st, [4sc, 2sc in the next st] 2x, 2sc (18).

Rnd 5: [5sc, 2sc in the next st] around (21).

Rnd 6: 3sc, 2sc in the next st, [6sc, 2sc in the next st] 2x, 3sc (24).

Rnd 7: [7sc, 2sc in the next st] around (27).

Rnds 8–11: 27sc (27).

Rnd 12: 8sc, crochet 1st EAR (ch7, 1hc in the 2nd st from hook, 3dc, 2hdc), 1sc in next st on HEAD, crochet 2nd EAR (see 1st EAR), 1sc in the next st on HEAD, 7sc.

Rnd 13: Change color to Cream, 8sc, 1sc over the 1st EAR, 10sc, 1sc over the 2nd EAR, 7sc (27).

Ch1 and turn, working in the opposite direction, so that the NUBS appear on the outside of the HEAD.

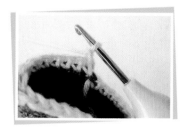

STONE
GRAY
(FB 242)

CREAM
(FB 130)

Rnd 14: [2sc, 1 nub (p. 109)] 9x (27).

Rnd 15: 27sc (27).

Rnd 16: [1 nub, 2sc] 9x (27).

Rnd 17: 13sc, 2sc in the next st, 13sc (28).

Rnd 18: 28sc (28).

Rnd 19: 8sc.

Stuff the HEAD with polyester filling.

Rnd 20: Crochet the HEAD together (see p. 10): 2sc in the next st, 11sc, 2sc in the next st (15).

Body

Work the BODY in rows, working along the 11 sts left at the bottom of the HEAD.

Row 1: Change color to Stone Gray, crochet 1st LEG (ch11, 1dc in the 3rd st from hook, 7dc, 4dc in the next st).

Change color to Cream, 15sc along the BODY (pull the 1st st tightly in order to fuse the LEG to the BODY).

Change color to Stone Gray, crochet 2nd LEG (see 1st LEG).

Row 2: Change color to Cream, 15sc along the BODY (15).

Rows 3–57: ch2, 1hdc+1sc in the 1st st on BODY, 14sc (16). Leave the last st of the 4th row unworked.

Row 58: ch2, 1hdc+1sc in the 1st st on BODY, 12sc, sc2tog (15).

Row 59: ch2, 1hdc+1sc in the 1st st on BODY, 11sc, sc2tog (14).

Row 60: ch2, 1hdc+1sc in the 1st st on BODY, 10sc, sc2tog (13).

Row 61: ch1, 12sc (12).

Row 62: Change color to Stone Gray, ch1, crochet 3rd LEG (1sc, ch11, 1dc in the 3rd st from hook, 8dc, 1sc in the next st on BODY), change color to Cream, [1sc, ch2, 1sc in the next st on BODY] 4x.

Change color to Stone Gray, crochet 4th LEG (see 3rd LEG).

Eyes

Work Variation 1 of the EYES (see p. 10).

Finishing

Sew the EYES 3 rows below the color change on the HEAD, 1st apart from each other. Weave in ends.

Harrison Hare

...has a big family

Advanced Memory Workouts
to Navigate
Your Family Reunion

SIZE: ABOUT 13.5 INCHES

RED
(FB 396)

WHITE
(FB 106)

BLACK
(FB 110)

GOLD
(FB 249)

APPLE
GREEN
(FB 205)

TAUPE
(FB 254)

Head

Work the HEAD in Taupe in a spiral round.

Rnd 1: 6sc in a magic ring (6).

Rnd 2: 2sc in every st (12).

Rnd 3: [1sc, 2sc in the next st] around (18).

Rnd 4: 1sc, 2sc in the next st, [2sc, 2sc in the next st] 5x, 1sc (24).

Rnd 5: [3sc, 2sc in the next st] around (30).

Rnds 6–10: 30sc (30).

Rnd 11: 1sc, ch15, reinsert the hook in the 16th st from the start of the ch, being careful not to twist the ch, 14sc (30).

Rnd 12: 30sc (30).

Rnd 13: [sc3, sc2tog] around (24).

Rnd 14: 24sc (24).

Rnd 15: [sc2, sc2tog] around (18).

Rnds 16+17: 18sc (18).

Rnd 18: 3sc.

Rnd 19: Crochet the HEAD together (see p. 10): sc2tog, 4sc, sc2tog (6).

Cut the yarn, leaving a long tail, and pull it through the last st to fasten off. The MOUTH will be sewn to the HEAD later.

Tongue

Work the TONGUE in Red in rows.

Row 1: ch4.

Row 2: 1dc in the 3rd st from the hook, dc (2).

Cut the yarn, leaving a long tail, and pull it through the last st to fasten off. Using a yarn needle, pull one end through the middle of the MOUTH. Pull the other end through a st next to the middle of the MOUTH. Knot the ends together on the wrong side of the MOUTH and trim.

Teeth (2X)

Work the TEETH in White in rows.

Row 1: ch3.

Row 2: dc in the 3rd st from the hook.

Cut the yarn, leaving a long tail, and pull it through the last st to fasten off. Attach the TEETH similarly to the TONGUE, attaching one end to the last round of the MOUTH and the other one st across.

Stuff the top and bottom halves of the HEAD with stuffing and fit the MOUTH inside, between the top and bottom

Mouth

Work the MOUTH in Black in a spiral round.

Rnd 1: 6sc in a magic ring (6).

Rnd 2: 2sc in every st (12).

Rnd 3: [1sc, 2sc in the next st] around (18).

Rnd 4: 1sc, 2sc in the next st, [2sc, 2sc in the next st] 5x, 1sc (24).

Rnd 5: [3sc, 2sc in the next st] around (30).

lips of the HEAD. Sew through both loops of the MOUTH sts and only the back loop of the HEAD sts.

Body

Work the BODY in Taupe in rows, working along the 6 sts left at the bottom of the HEAD.

Row 1: ch1, 3sc into the next st, 4sc, 3sc into the next st (10).

Row 2: ch1, 2sc into the next st, 8sc, 2sc into the next st, crochet 1st LEG (see LEGS instructions to the right).

Row 3: 3sc into the next st, 11sc, crochet 2nd LEG.

Row 4: 3sc into the next st, 11sc (14).

Rows 5–63: ch1, 12sc (12).

Row 64: ch1, sc2tog, 8sc, sc2tog (10).

Row 65: ch1, 1sc, crochet 3rd LEG, 1sc into the next st on the BODY, 7sc, crochet 4th LEG, 1sc in the next st on the BODY.

Cut the yarn, leaving a long tail, and pull it through the last st to fasten off. Weave in ends.

Legs (4x)

Continue working in Taupe without cutting the yarn.

Row 1: ch14, [ch4, 1hdc in the 3rd st from the hook, 1hdc] 4x.

Rnd 17: [1sc, 2sc into the next st] 4x, 1sc (13).

Cut the yarn, leaving a long tail, and pull it through the last st to fasten off. You'll sew the ears onto the head later.

Ears (2x)

Work the EARS in Taupe in a spiral round.

Rnd 1: 4sc in a magic ring (4).

Rnd 2: 2sc in each st (8).

Rnd 3: [1sc, 2sc into the next st] around (12).

Rnd 4: [2sc, 2sc into the next st] 4x (16).

Rnds 5–9: 16sc (16).

Rnd 10: sc2tog, 6sc, sc2tog, 6sc (14).

Rnd 11: sc2tog, 12sc (13).

Rnd 12: sc2tog, 11sc (12).

Rnd 13: sc2tog, 10sc (11).

Rnd 14: sc2tog, 9sc (10).

Rnd 15: sc2tog, 8sc (9).

Rnd 16: 9sc (9).

Carrot

Work the CARROT in Gold in a spiral round. First, prepare the carrot greens. Cut a few 4" strands of Apple Green and knot them together in the middle.

Rnd 1: Work 6sc in a magic ring.

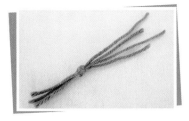

Before you pull the magic ring closed, lay the carrot greens in the hole so the knot lies on the inner side.

Insert the hook from the left into the last–worked TOE, wrap the yarn and pull through. Do this for all of the TOES. You'll have 5 loops on your hook.

Wrap the yarn and pull through all 5 loops.

Row 2: 14sc along the ch.

Pull the ring closed so that the greens are secure, then continue to crochet (6).

Rnds 2–5: 6sc (6).

Rnd 6: sc2tog, 4sc (5).

Rnds 7+8: 5sc (5).

Cut the yarn, leaving a long tail, and pull it through the last st to fasten off. Sew the carrot closed and trim the yarn.

Eyes

Work Variation 2 of the EYES (see p. 11).

Finishing

Sew the EYES to the HEAD one row over the top lip, with the narrowest part between them 2 sts apart. Next, sew the EARS to the HEAD one row over the EYES. Sew the CARROT to one of the HANDS using a Taupe thread; wrap the fingers around the carrot.

For the TAIL, wrap White yarn over 3 tines of a fork. Wrap a piece of Taupe yarn around the middle of the White wrapped strands and knot to secure. Remove the bundle from the fork and cut open the looped ends of the White yarn to make a pompom. Trim the pompom evenly. Using the Taupe thread, sew the pompom between the bottom LEGS on the BODY.

Guide to Schachenmayr Yarns by Color Number

Name	Number	Name	Number
White	106	Linen	248
Black	110	Gold	249
Cream	130	Hot Pink	252
Peacock Blue	146	Taupe	254
Chestnut	157	Raspberry	256
Coffee	162	Soft Apricot	263
Silver	172	Terracotta	388
Wine	192	Red	396
Apple Green	205	Mauve	399
Khaki	212	Sand	404
Green	241	Pink	409
Stone Gray	242	Garnet	413
Light Pink	246		